*By Water
and the
Holy Spirit*

BY WATER
AND THE
HOLY SPIRIT

*New Concepts of Baptism,
Confirmation,
and Communion*

JOHN M. HINES

Foreword by Alfred R. Shands

A Crossroad Book   THE SEABURY PRESS · NEW YORK

Copyright © 1973 by The Seabury Press, Inc.
ISBN: 0-8164-5703-4
Text and Cover Design by Carol Basen
Printed in the United States of America

Foreword

This short book is, I suppose, a sequel to *How and Why* which Barry Evans and I wrote two years ago for Seabury Press. Judging by the positive response our book received, it was clear that many within the Episcopal Church were ready for some practical help in how best to use the new liturgies of the Eucharist and the Daily Office. *Services for Trial Use*—the "Green Book"—came on the Church with amazingly little preparation. Though there had been a long preparation for the services among a small minority of the Church, most of the clergy and laity were quite unprepared to use and evaluate these services they were asked by their bishops to use and evaluate. The results in many cases ran anywhere from frustration to apathy. It is my feeling that even now that *Services for Trial Use* has had a two-year exposure in the parish church, the need for adequate preparation is as important as ever. Perhaps it was thought somewhat naively that the new services would in time teach themselves. I do not think this has happened. The only parishes I know of where the new services of Eucharist and Morning Prayer have caught on are parishes where a considerable effort has been made with the congregation to convey the meaning and spirit of worship. Otherwise the new forms in the green book tend to feel like ill-fitting and uncomfortable clothes.

If the new forms of the Eucharist and Morning Prayer which we use each Sunday are still foreign to many parishes, how much more remote must the new form of Baptism and Laying on of Hands be. In my own parish I can recall encountering this new service only three or four times on Sunday morning. Most of the congregation had never seen the service before, and the result was what might be expected—confusion.

All of this only says "Amen" to the importance of what John Hines has attempted in this book—to prepare the parish for the new rite of Baptism. I would add a second "Amen" to his approach to the subject—the experience of children. Somehow the ability of children to participate in worship remains the surest ground of the validity of adult worship. If the experience of worship is coming through on the level of the immediacy, enthusiasm, and gaiety of children, then it is probably reaching us on our most basic level. The inability of the parish to take children seriously in the action of parish worship results in the kind of abstractness and boredom which we all know too well on Sunday morning.

John Hines is a person well qualified to write from his chosen point of view, for not only has he been a parish priest with the responsibility of the Sunday School, but he also faces a class of twenty children each day in the school where he teaches ninth grade. He is a gifted teacher with imagination and ingenuity.

What this study guide requires is a community of people who really care—who care about what worship means to their parish; who care that they themselves have experienced Baptism into Christ and have been sealed by the Spirit; who care what worship means to children. Such a community, no matter how small, can use this book to great advantage. They will discover that liturgical renewal is far more than substituting service B for service A, no matter how desirable the changes may be. The changes are only a gateway to a wider and deeper awareness of God.

ALFRED R. SHANDS

Contents

Introduction

"Parents, teach your children well . . .
Children, teach your parents well . . .
. . . and know they love you."

—*Crosby, Stills, Nash, and Young.*

Perhaps this book is not so much about Baptism, Confirmation and Communion as it is about children in the Church and our response as adults to them.

At the Episcopal Church's General Convention of 1970, a resolution was passed which allowed, at the discretion of the diocesan bishop, any baptized person to participate fully in the Holy Eucharist. This action by the Episcopal Church had three important results. It affirmed the fullness of Baptism as an initiation rite, saying that baptized persons should not be discouraged from receiving the Church's central sacrament: "Baptism means *full* membership." Secondly, it resulted in a closer look at Confirmation. If one can receive Communion without being confirmed, what is the meaning of Confirmation? Convention's resolution has called on the Church to reevaluate, and in reality to reemphasize, the main point of Confirmation; namely the occasion when a baptized member can make his or her own decision toward a personal commitment to the Christian enterprise.

The third effect of the resolution is that because Baptism, early Communion, and Confirmation generally involve children and young adults, we must begin to deal with these younger members of the Church within the context of the entire congregation. In other words, instead of restricting children and young people into lesser positions in the Church, or neglecting them entirely, we now must observe their roles in a new light.

So this book is really about children in the Church. And the instruments used to examine that issue are the rites of Baptism and Confirmation, and the reception of the Eucharist by nonconfirmed members.

This book has a bias. It is that children are people— small, young people to be sure, but God's people! Adults have the responsibility both to bring up those children in the best of the Christian tradition and to learn from them. Our children learn from watching us act. We must learn from their actions as well.

One very valid question at this point in Episcopal Church history might be "What is the status of this Baptism/Confirmation rite?" In 1970, the Convention passed a resolution enabling the use of the service of Baptism with the laying-on-of-hands. However, there were definite conditions as to how the service was to be conducted. More than a little confusion has surfaced because of this fact. The Green Book service has definite aspects which need revision and there is little doubt that these revisions will have been presented at the General Convention in Louisville, Kentucky, in 1973. The House of Bishops and the Standing Liturgical Commission continue to urge the use of the existing rite—which brings up another point.

For many years the Book of Common Prayer has been the primary source of Episcopal theology, which may explain some negative reactions to the Green Book. The theology of Prayer-Book revision is different in some areas from that of the 1928 Prayer Book. Indeed, on such issues as membership, sacramental relationships, the rule of the Church, the 1928 Prayer Book's stance has been expanded. Not only has practice been changed—early Communion, for example—but new theology is being revealed. This means there may be some people who are being made uncomfortable. It also means that the Church is entering an exciting new era of its life. Excitement brings tension, just as tension brings excitement and new possibilities.

In essence, what has happened is that we have been challenged to practice what we have preached. We have said that Baptism is full membership in the Church. We have said that the Eucharist is our central act of praise and thanksgiving, a common union for all Christians. We have claimed that Confirmation is a personal decision to accept a commitment. But unfortunately, we have practiced Baptism as a nice thing to have done, excluded some baptized members from the Holy Communion, and made Confirmation a completion of Baptism and a ticket to the Eucharist. We must re-think our position and the focus for that re-thinking should be on the children.

To look at it from another point of view, one might see our present task as preparing our children for Baptism, Communion, and the laying-on-of-hands. But before we can instruct others, we must study how we ourselves feel about these things. Then when we talk to our children about an issue, we will be able to learn from them in return. There is no better way to learn than to try to teach.

In treating of initiation rites and this reevaluation process, this book will make certain assumptions. The first and most important assumption is that people in the Church are concerned and responsible. "People" means lay as well as clergy. In fact, this book is not a theological book but is aimed at the interested lay person—which leads to a second assumption.

Theology grows out of and is formed from experience and action. We act in faith and as a response to what we perceive as God's will, and theology follows. The Last Supper did not require a theology. It required people gathering, sharing, eating, and drinking. No doubt the disciples had little understanding of any theological basis for that meal. Only later, after the experience, only after Easter did the followers begin to understand. They theologized *after* they participated. Doing comes first, theology follows. A hungry child needs to be fed, not instructed about the value of nutrition. Just as, in the old phrase, "A drowning man needs a life preserver, not swimming lessons." Certainly we often have a theological foundation for our actions, but theology is no prerequisite for them.

This book deals with practical observations and resources more than with theological truths. It contains some recorded reactions from people about Baptism, Communion, and Confirmation. There are some liturgical suggestions and a look at the Green Book rite of Baptism with the laying-on-of-hands. It tries to say that what is important about worship is not the Prayer Book or the Green Book but a combination of how we do the service and an awareness of why we are doing it. Some congregations are finding out that renewal does not grow out of a form but out of an awareness and a response to that awareness. In order to take advantage of the new possibilities set before us we must not worry about doing things "correctly," but about doing them well.

> Teach your parents well . . .
> Teach your children well . . .
> . . . and know they love you.

JOHN M. HINES

Maundy Thursday, 1973

CHAPTER *1*

The Cycle

Once upon a time, there came into existence an individual named "E." When E was a few months old, E's parents decided to have E baptized. After Baptism, E grew up "in the Episcopal Church," looking forward to that occasion on which E would be made a full member and, upon reaffirming and thereby completing the vows of Baptism in Confirmation, be admitted to the Holy Communion.

Between Baptism and Confirmation, E experienced choir and Sunday School and served a brief stint with the acolytes and Episcopal Young Churchmen (EYC). Upon reaching the age of twelve, E attended Confirmation class at the "urging" of Mr. and Mrs. E and because Sunday School for an eighth-grader was Confirmation class. The main direction of the class, at least in E's mind, was toward an understanding of the Creed and Communion. E's interest, already seriously damaged by Sunday School and choir, now began to dwindle even more. The classes had little to do with what E was really interested in, namely the everyday events of a twelve-year-old. Then there was a brief upsurge in E when the actual Confirmation took place. The bishop was there at the First Communion, a big, long service—yet the whole affair passed somewhere far above (or below) E's head.

Now starts the rapid delcline of E's involvement with the Church and the Church's involvement with E. High school came and went. E became an EYC dropout. E stopped going to Sunday School. ("I've already been confirmed.") And the services did not seem of interest. There were other concerns for E: dating, driver's license, drugs, voting, and college. Off to the university to return at Christmas and maybe attend the midnight service. College began to spark E's spiritual curiosity. A course in comparative religion, one on death, another about the occult. E got closer to "religion" and further away from the Church. An attempt to get involved with the local Canterbury Club proved disastrous for E.

Graduation presented E with the prospects of job-getting, then marriage to be followed by taxes, housing, and more. If E's parish was lucky—meaning if there was enough pressure from Mrs. E—the wedding took place at the church, but after the wedding the rector heard little from Mr. and Mrs. E until one day, a year or two later, E and E's spouse had a baby: E, Jr. (nicknamed "e"). Mr. and Mrs. E supposed that they "really ought to have young e baptized," and after remembering the name of the church, they called the parish to make arrangements. Two weeks later the Baptism was performed, privately. The Church had a new member, and the cycle was completed—or was it just beginning again?

This little story may be a bit exaggerated and touched with sarcasm, but unfortunately the essence of it is all too familiar to many Episcopal churches. There is a definite decline in a person's involvement in the Church after Confirmation. The problem is a cycle the Church has allowed and often encouraged to take place. That cycle is an ellipse with Baptism and Confirmation as its foci. This closed path, 'round and 'round, has long been the symbol for the role of children and young people in the Church. What was begun in Baptism is finished with Confirmation, and then the path bends backward instead of continuing forward. "I got the feeling that being confirmed was what the parish really wanted from me." This is a response from a fifteen-year-old when asked what her Confirmation meant to her. Another fifteen-year-old said, "I think Confirmation gave me something I didn't have before—it wasn't just the chance to take Communion but it was also the chance to be a member of the Church like my parents are." An eighteen-year-old recalls, "I felt stupid after Confirmation. I mean a couple of years later, when things weren't very different at all. I realize now that I didn't even know why I went into that Confirmation class." "Well, I hadn't thought much about it—before you asked—but I guess my Confirmation was about as important to me as my Baptism. I mean—I can't remember anything about either one."

These were a few opinions from young people who are still, at least periodically, involved with the Church. This is not to say that Confirmation has no value; for some kids, truly important changes came about because of their experience in a Confirmation class. The point is that the vast majority of young people between fourteen and twenty years old feel that Confirmation was something that was "done to them" rather than something they chose to do on their own. The predominant feeling is that of being caught up in the cycle of Church membership, doing the same things from Sunday to Sunday, reaching the age of Confirmation, being confirmed, and going on. A feeling of never really being moved toward a decision but always being acted upon, always passively accepting until the day "I don't have to go anymore."

And yet there are many parishes and missions where children, young people and old people are excited about what they are doing. They feel that they are a part of the action, not simply on the receiving end. Many of these congregations have stressed three things: (1) the importance of Baptism, (2) the receiving of Communion before Confirmation, and (3) a Confirmation class that amounts to lay ordination or commitment, where the individual is in the class because he or she has decided to be there and is ready to make some very real sacrifices and promises.

Breaking the Cycle

Such churches demonstrate that the death-dealing cycle of Baptism-Confirmation-(marriage)-Baptism can be broken. The Christian view of history has always been a progressive one, linear and developing; not cyclical, repetitious, with no chance for something new. It is a great tragedy that during the years when a person is most inquisitive and is in need of recognition and guidance, the Church fails, indeed often refuses to try to be a resource.

The 1970 General Convention has placed before every diocese and each congregation the opportunity to be that resource. The Green Book Services of Baptism and the laying-on-of-hands, along with the concept of early Communion, (a horrible term), provide occasions for cycle-breaking and renewal.

Renewal will not come easily. Renewal implies there was something new there in the first place which now needs building up. When most pre-Confirmation children are asked about Communion, their answers reflect a pathetic situation common to many congregations. "I don't know what happens after we leave except they have the sermon and *the Communion.* Sometimes I stay and get a blessing." When a fifth-grader was asked about Baptism, she answered, "Last year we had one during the 9:30 service and they (the clergy) walked around showing the baby to everybody. It was neat! But we only did that once."

Immediately after a Baptism in a typical Episcopal church, a ten-year-old boy replied, "It sounded like fun but I couldn't see much." Our children are suffering from a serious case of under exposure. Many children say that they are not interested in Baptism, Communion, or Confirmation and too often it is because they see no excitement on the part of the adults who participate. "It doesn't look to me like they're really happy about it. Everyone looks so sad." Before we can renew Baptism, Confirmation, and Communion for our children, we must be convinced of their value ourselves. One of the great byproducts of trying to teach someone something is that to do a good job of it you must first come to grips with the subject yourself. Preparing children for Baptism, Communion, and Confirmation means preparing ourselves.

"Roger and I had to try to answer some really hard questions about Communion when we sat down with the girls. They asked things I've wanted to ask for a long time, like why do they put water into the wine? If it is supposed to be a meal, why do we kneel? Why this? Why that? And we realized we didn't know a darn thing about the Communion service." This from a mother of three children who has been an Episcopalian for thirty-six years. How often do we take time before a service to think what we are about to participate in? In many parishes where a special Sunday's Communion service was designed to be the "First Communion" for un-confirmed people, the parents and other adults profited more from the service than did the kids.

We must re-evaluate in our own minds what the great sacraments mean to us and there is no better way to learn than to teach.

How Children Learn

Any discussion of children's involvement in the Church must be accompanied by an investigation of how children learn. This is particularly true for the Church because for a long time this institution has not concentrated on her children: how they develop, what they think and what affects them.

As a matter of fact our culture for hundreds of years has taken to its heart the saying, "children should be seen and not heard." Only recently has the area of child psychology and sociology been discovered. More specifically and more recently the dimensions of children and how they learn has opened up and revealed some interesting studies. In the educational/behavioral area names like Simon, Kozol, Neill, Illich, Holt, Silberman, and Herndon have surfaced. These men and many others have, through their interest and concern for children and education, thrown some new light on the rather dark scenes of children's learnings.

Two of the main figures on the psychology side of children and learning are Harvard's Jerome Bruner and Swiss psychologist Jean Piaget.

For many years our attitude toward learning could be summed up in the phrase which almost all of us have heard at one time or another, "Unless you can express it (write it or orally articulate it) you really do not understand what you have 'learned'." Verbal or written communication was for all purposes the only barometer in evaluating a child's understanding. In school the student was presented with an amount of material which he was to eventually understand. After a period of time the teacher would give an examination which would show how much the student understood. Of course most tests were designed to see what the child did *not* know! Many of us as students were able to memorize material, repeat the memorization on paper during an exam, and after having been christened ("he understands") by means of a passing grade, promptly forgot almost everything we had been assigned. We were rarely, if ever, taught the concepts upon which our material was based, but even when we were, the method of evaluating that knowledge was almost always that of the written word. "If you understand it then you can say it; if you can say it then you can write it." The basic assumption was that the adult verbal manner, rational and relatively mature, was the model by which children's understanding was judged.

The pathetic and disturbing fact is that in spite of new discoveries this same attitude is still at the heart of the great majority of our educational systems which deal with children. We still evaluate them as small adults and do not recognize their non-verbal and supra-rational development. The fact that children *do* learn concepts long before they are able to articulate that learning is precisely what men like Bruner and Piaget are trying to tell us. This "conceptual understanding" may well begin at birth. Some say even before birth. At any rate, recent studies reveal that understanding of concepts begins and continues on many different levels of a child's development in addition to the level of fairly explicit verbal

expression, that level usually occurring at age twelve—
the "magic age."

In the past when we said that the child did not understand something the chances are that it was not that the
child did not understand but that he simply had not
developed the ability to exercise the skill of expressing
his understanding in a rational, verbal, adult manner.
The Church has done the same thing as far as the nonconfirmed person's receiving communion is concerned. It
was generally held that unless a person could express his
understanding of the sacrament, it was not available to
him. The articulation of the understanding was Confirmation, the rite in which the child became an adult
Christian.

Now, however, Piaget and Bruner, along with General
Convention's resolution concerning "early Communion,"
have changed things. Piaget holds that his studies show
that eighteen-month-old children are capable of recognizing and using images and symbols in creating some
kind of order to deal with the world they experience. He
goes on to describe in detail the different levels of understanding and articulation a child experiences.

Bruner suggests that conceptual material can be effectively transmitted in some intellectually honest form to
any child at any stage of his development.

General Convention's resolution of 1970 has given
the Church an opportunity to put Piaget's and Bruner's
findings into practice. If a child is allowed and encouraged to take Communion with some regularity and is
accepted as a full member of the congregation, he is
quite capable of understanding the basic concepts of the
Eucharist—giving, receiving, sharing, and being thank-
ful. Other more complex concepts such as forgiveness
and sacrifice can be taught and experienced with a little

extra effort. Furthermore the great value of a child's participation in this central act of the Church is that the experience will be invaluable when he does reach the level of verbal expression. From experience a theology can grow.

Children in Church

Just as our culture has underestimated the abilities which children possess, our Church has done the very same thing. Ironically, however, the Church seems to be the one institution in which children can be accepted as real people and given the value and respect due them. We have scriptural reference to children and what important people they are. We are told to be like them and to embody many of their attributes. We read that we all are the children of God. And yet we have turned right around and treated our children as second-class Christians, unconsciously perhaps, but we have done it nonetheless. We have taken little interest in church school education, using Sunday School more as a Sunday morning day care center than as an opportunity to involve our children in some meaningful activities and learnings. Most of our Sunday School teachers really do not and are not able to keep up with new findings in education and child psychology. Most teachers are volunteers or retired school teachers and often rely totally on past experience to pull them through another year.

In the Sunday service itself the children are usually herded out before the Service is over. Unfortunately, this exodus is usually a good thing because the service is so aimed at the adult in the congregation that the children would simply die of boredom in the pews. The general atmosphere which pervades the majority of

Episcopal churches is so "reverent" that the children are scared to death of doing something wrong, like dropping the nickel their parents gave them for the offertory. There is no more pitiful sight than that of a young acolyte trying desperately to put out a candle which towers four feet over his head. He becomes frustrated and increasingly petrified because the adults are waiting for him to do his job and he is afraid of failing.

A bit overstated? Perhaps not in the eyes of children involved in a Sunday service whose tradition is that things go smoothly and correctly. They have been, and continue to be, caught between being treated like infants and having expectations, some of which are of adult proportions, placed on.them. It is no wonder that children themselves have no idea what their role in the Church is. On the one hand they feel insignificant, on the other they experience tremendous pressures to be "grown up."

What about a solution? There are many different approaches to the problem but the first step is one of awareness. We must become sensitive to our children. We must become aware of their feelings. We must try to understand the effect we adults have upon our children. A child, like everyone else, learns through experience and imitation. An expert in children's education was asked by an adult class one Sunday, "What is Christian education?" The man thought a moment then spoke of an episode he had just witnessed during the service which preceded the class. It was a family service, and while the lesson was being read he noticed two adults carrying on a conversation, paying no attention to the reading. "That," the man said, "is Christian education." The children watching those two adults learned about church. They may not have learned accurately, but they learned. We must first become aware of the children around us and become aware that they are continually learning.

"I can vividly remember being very young and thinking, 'Church is a place where people go to be sad'," says an eighteen-year-old college freshman. "I have never taken children in church very seriously. I guess it's because I felt I was never taken very seriously when I was one." Adults must become aware of and sensitive to children.

Once children are recognized the natural step would be to include them in the action and begin to tailor at least parts of the services to young people. Parishes, for example, which have instituted children's sermons by the clergy during the service have discovered that not only the children but the adults as well learn from such presentations. "I wish Father ____ would talk to us like he talks to the kids," replied a parent. "I can understand his kid-speak."

The danger we run here is that of *tokenism* or treating children as children — separate from the rest of the congregation. That is why children's chapels and youth services have problems. They can become performances whereby we recognize our children but avoid really including them in the family. Like little Mary Ellen who is paraded out to play the piano for guests some evening, we can use our children in church the same way. However, child tokenism is better than child neglect.

Another item in services which can include children is music; music they can recognize and sing. Once again, children are not to be underestimated. When one mentions children's music, thoughts of "Onward Christian Soldiers" and "Jesus Loves Me" spring to mind. Kids dislike the childish hymns and songs just as much as the music which is so foreign to them that it makes no sense at all. Young people do not want all guitar music either. They are interested in learning about church music, its history and its future, but not as "knowledge necessary for salvation." Junior choirs can be very good instruments of learning for children, offering them an opportunity for real participation. But what often happens is that when the big day comes — Easter, Christmas, Pentecost—the children get left out. Another problem with junior or youth choirs is that church music has had a tradition of excellence. Whether church music has actually been excellent or not is another matter—but the tradition is that music in church, like behavior, should be proper. Therefore children's choirs are seldom given a chance to do their thing because the music director fears a "bad performance." The question which must be asked is, what comes first, musical excellence or the participation of children in church? As we bring children into honest involvement with the Church there will be occasions in which we, as adults, will have to change our behavior and attitude. Sacrificing musical excellence for real involvement of children is one such situation.

Another situation which will require some effort on the part of adults in order to help the children learn about church and themselves is the issue of noise. Centuries of tradition have resulted in the practice of silence in church. When we begin to take our younger members seriously enough to have them stay throughout a service we are also going to have to accept the accompanying results. It is a fact that children talk. They also drop things and they giggle. The basic fact is that children in church are quite frank about their behavior. They have not fully learned to stifle their feelings or reactions just because they are in church. And because children pattern their behavior after adults, it does not take a child long to accept the "silence is reverence" motto and slip into the same catatonic state his parents do upon entering the church. The cure? Congregations can relax. Yes, children should learn what is acceptable behavior in church and what is not, but a person himself should not have to be any different in church than anywhere else.

Children and the Sacraments

We have briefly investigated how children learn and how that learning relates to their experience in church in general. Now we will take a broad look at children and their relationship to Communion, Baptism and Confirmation.

There seem to be two general ways of looking at the sacraments. One way emphasizes the person's intellectual ability to understand as well as his faith. The other way stresses the dependence upon God to make the sacrament a powerful force despite the weaknesses in intellect and faith of the recipient. Needless to say, both God's action and our ability to respond are necessary to the making of a sacrament but the question is which to stress?

Certainly no one can claim that he or she fully understands Baptism or Communion. Certainly the disciples had little idea of the meaning of the events which went on at the Last Supper. They had no theological understanding of the Eucharist. It was only after they had shared bread and wine with Jesus, after His death, that their experience became clear to them. One can imagine the reaction of the disciples after Easter morning. "Yes, that was what He said. Now it all begins to make sense." Neither did they fully intellectualize nor really understand the idea of going out with the word to baptize in the name of the Holy Trinity. That task and the experience of the first Eucharist were not dependent upon any ability to fully comprehend the concepts behind them.

We know now that infants and children understand much more than we used to think they did. Of course, a six-year-old is not as able to deal with Holy Communion as an eighteen-year-old. But do we say that in order to participate in a Eucharist you must be able to understand it? Is that the requirement? If so, then there are many of us who are cheating on the requirements!

What's more, if one believes in infant baptism, as the Anglican Church does, wherein grace and benefit are given during a rite of which the recipient is totally unconscious, how then can one fail to claim the same process at Holy Communion without displaying a gross inconsistency? If an infant's sponsors and community are responsible for the baptismal vows, why cannot the congregation be responsible in the development of a child's idea of Communion through experiencing the meal?

Recently a diocese asked some of its clergy about the practice of admitting nonconfirmed people—children—to Communion. Here is a sampling of the responses:

"Infants and young children lack sufficient understanding for repentance, faith, and receiving the sacrament."

"The practice would negate the teachings of the Church for many years."

"Participation in Holy Communion requires at least some intellectual involvement above the childish level."

"It (early Communion) would make a liar out of me in the eyes of all these people whom I have taught differently."

"A small child has no sense of remembrance as used in the Prayer of Consecration. A child has no understanding of Incarnation. A child has little sense of obligation, especially in the solemnity of the celebration of Holy Eucharist; nor does he have a sense of anamnesis."

From statements like these it does not take much work to conclude that many people in the Church simply do not consider infants, young children, or even adolescents as real members of the Body of Christ. Generally, people regard the child's role in the Church to be one of "cuteness." We enjoy children in church but we rarely accept them as the full-fledged baptized Christians they are. We exclude them from most of the Baptism service either by having private Baptisms or by not taking a little time to arrange things so the children in the congregation can see and participate in what's going on. We have excluded them from the Church's central act of worship. And when we have allowed them to "do their thing," it is usually at five o'clock some Sunday afternoon or early in the morning. All too often we see it as "the children's service" and comment on "how cute they were" and "isn't it nice they had a chance to perform at our service."

Children, infants, and adolescents have a very important and valid role in the Church. If they have been baptized, they are full members and should be allowed all the rights, privileges, and responsibilities of that membership. Their role is the same as all our roles— sharing, caring, learning, growing, being sorry and forgiving, loving one another as Christ loved us. There is no second-class citizenry in that role. There are no exclusive requirements save that of professing Jesus Christ as Lord.

"... Like Little Children ..."

Perhaps the most important role that children have in the Church is that of making us adults wake up. Jesus recognized children and their potential as resources. "Be like them," He said. He meant notice them, learn from them, accept them. It is the adults who are usually supposed to be responsible for the children's growth and development. But we need to turn that process around every so often to recapture in ourselves the honesty, the good aspects of innocence and naïvete that we see in our children. We have the opportunities for recognizing children's roles in Baptism, in the laying-on-of-hands, and in the Holy Eucharist. The cycle can be broken. Children are people; and even we old adults can be taught new tricks.

Finally, when dealing with children in the church, *don't organize them!* Children definitely do need time to be with their peer group, developing their own theology and relationships. They need to learn to be with other kids. But they also need to learn to be with the larger community in the context of the whole congregation. We too often organize children out of our adult existence. We have children's chapels and children's choirs to the exclusion of their participation in the larger community. And then sometimes we allow them to come into *our* service, to do their little thing and then disappear, maybe to return next year. To be involved in the congregation, children must be recognized and trusted. Children, like women, have suffered in the Church from lack of recognition. Children as well as women can be ushers, bring up the communion elements, read lessons, and do a host of things which only men usually do. We must trust children to participate, and through that participation to learn what the Church is like. It is only then that enthusiasm, real enthusiasm, develops, not when it has been "organized" to happen. And probably the most valuable occasion for children's participation, experiencing, and learning is at the Holy Eucharist. If the Communion is as important to us as we say it is then we must share that importance with our children.

Just as younger children must be allowed their place in the Church through Baptism and the receiving of Communion, so must young adults be given the opportunity to study and decide about their commitment to the Church. We can't "organize" them into Confirmation classes they don't want to be in, but we must provide opportunities for them to investigate what commitment means. Sessions centered around such questions as Why is commitment necessary? What would it entail? Why haven't we lived up to our commitments (for those who have already been confirmed)? People desiring to receive the laying-on-of-hands might be asked to make an initial commitment to attend classes or enter a kind of apprenticeship of confirmand-in-training situation. The main point that has to be explained is that this decision is a serious one, arrived at by the individual and supported by the parish.

CHAPTER *2*

The Service

It is amazing how many people, both lay and clerical, have never read through the Green Book. Of course not many of us have ever read through the Prayer Book either, but *Services For Trial Use,* as its title says, is meant for us to *use* on a trial basis. When you use something you should examine it and find out why it is the way it is before you try to evaluate it. Every Episcopalian, liturgically minded or not, ought to sit down with a copy of the Green Book and read it from cover to cover. It does not take very long and the exercise will be a surprising enlightenment.

Such a reading is especially valuable for the service of Holy Baptism with the Laying-on-of-Hands. Much has been said about this service, liturgically and theologically. Some of the most common questions are: "Who can perform the service?" "Is it true that the laying-on-of-hands can only be done by a bishop?" "Who made the decision about this early Communion idea?" "What is the story on who gets the laying-on-of-hands and at what age?" The answer to all these can be found in the explanation on page 21 of the Green Book. This explanation is the enabling resolution of the 63rd General Convention.

In Houston in 1970 there was much discussion by the House of Bishops concerning this rite. As the resolution states, the service was accepted only after it was amended so that the laying-on-of-hands would still correspond to the traditional age of Confirmation. In other words, although the Convention stated that nonconfirmed baptized persons could receive Communion it also stipulated that only those of "The present age normal for confirmation (or older) shall receive the laying-on-of-hands. . . ." Many at Houston argued that the service of Baptism with the laying-on-of-hands administered to an infant would replace and also destroy the rite of Confirmation as an adult affirmation of faith. Once everything was "completed" by this service for an infant, how would an individual express his decision to make a personal commitment similar to today's confirmation? There was present in Houston—and is still present today —a real fear of losing Confirmation.

But there is another way of looking at the new rite and that is by recognizing that the idea of baptism with laying-on-of-hands could force us to come up with a renewed and up-dated service of commitment modeled along the lines of lay ordination. In other words, instead of losing Confirmation, we would be expanding and regenerating it! The present service of Commitment (p. 327 Green Book) while at least providing the idea of individual renewal, does not fulfill (and was not designed to fulfill) the idea of lay ordination or Confirmation.

As for the service itself, there are helpful suggestions and directions for the service of Holy Baptism with the laying-on-of-hands on pages 22, and from 32 to 33. They will answer many questions. The service begins on p. 23 with the greeting and response. One might note here that the Green Book Service is complete in itself from the beginning, whereas the Baptism rite in the Prayer Book was designed to be used within the context of another service, starting as it does with "Hath this Child been already baptized or no?"

The collect of the day follows the greeting and then the set collect for Baptism (p. 24) is said. The basic theme of Baptism—namely death and rebirth in Christ— is presented in this collect. As we shall see later, the symbol of water is the perfect image to carry out this life-death theme.

The Ministry of the Word consists of Scripture readings with possible selections from the Ezekiel, Second Corinthians, Romans, St. Mark, and St. John. This portion of the service is also a good time for using literary sources as well as biblical in effectively presenting the theme. More is said about this in a later chapter about liturgical suggestions.

The sermon follows and traditionally comments upon the reading of the Word, after which the clergy, candidates, and sponsors move to the font for the presentation and affirmations.

In this portion of the service a series of questions and responses on the part of the candidates, the sponsors, and the congregation culminates in one of the most innovative and exciting elements of the Baptism rite and of the Green Book as a whole. This is the saying of the Creed in the form of questions and responses. The previous questions and responses led naturally to the Creed and this new form (the text is recommended by the International Consultation on English texts) continues the "give and take." The Creed itself becomes a response, an active thing instead of a statement we memorize and repeat. It should be noted that historically the Creed as we know it came from the early Christian baptismal questions and answers.

A short litany for those to be baptized follows the Creed and it is effective to have a sponsor for it. The litany is another opportunity for response. The congregation instead of sitting and watching is drawn into the service, affirming and responding to what is being said and done. After all, Baptism is an opportunity for all baptized people to reaffirm their own promises.

Water is a very vivid and intricate symbol. The Green Book attempts in the Baptism service to offer an explanation of this symbol in the prayer, the Blessing of the Water. The prayer is a summation of what the whole rite is about and should be the liturgical focal point of the service. In this prayer the life and death imagery mentioned in the Baptism Collect (p. 24) is examined more deeply.

The water was present at Creation. It played an important role in the Israelites escape from Egypt, and it was the outer instrument in Jesus' baptism by John. In each example, water symbolizes both death and new life. The chaos of water in the beginning represents death out of which good formed order, which was life. The waters of the Red Sea drowned Pharoah's forces of oppression and slavery while giving a new life of freedom to the people of Israel. John's baptism of Jesus in the Jordan's water pointed Jesus toward the crucifixion and the resurrection.

The prayer says it beautifully, summing up the symbol in the great command to go out and baptize all nations.

While the Church has often talked about death and new life in Baptism it has occasionally neglected the symbol of water in explaining the death and life. This is apparent in the fact that most Episcopal churches have abandoned the practice of total immersion in water, an act representing a drowning death to sin as well as a rising to new life. The idea of drowning does not usually come to one's mind when the priest sprinkles water on the forehead of a candidate. Again, liturgical suggestions as to how the Baptism might be done effectively will be discussed in another chapter.

Oil of chrism is an historical expression of "sealing" the candidate after Baptism. It was used immediately after the Baptism by water and symbolized the strengthening of the newly formed bond. Such a seal closed the body from the devil's re-entry. In the early Christian Church the candidate was anointed before Baptism with the "oil of exorcism" and then, after rising from the water, with the "oil of thanksgiving."

Probably about the fourteenth century or so, the practice of anointing with oil became tied in with the developing rite of Confirmation and away from Baptism. It is from this tradition that the Green Book's use of oil of chrism comes. In other words, oil is used only in the laying-on-of-hands, not in Baptism.

According to General Convention's enabling resolution, the Baptism and laying-on-of-hands can only be administered to a person at least as old as those who have been presented for Confirmation in the past; the minimal age there being around eleven or twelve years old. Therefore, all infants are baptized using the baptismal portion of this rite and omitting the sections which deal with the laying-on-of-hands. This causes problems with the Green Book's initiation rites, which could be remedied by having one service of Baptism and another service of laying-on-of-hands. These could fit together or stand alone as needed.

On page 29 the minister takes the candidate and dips him in the water or pours the water on him, saying the traditional baptismal proclamation. Then the congregation joins the minister in a prayer for those baptized and for those to be confirmed.

At this point if there are candidates for Confirmation they come before the bishop and he lays his hands on them and makes the sign of the cross on their foreheads, using oil which he may have blessed or not, as he wished. He declares that the candidates are sealed by the Holy Spirit. According to the enabling resolution, only the bishop can perform this portion of the service. The rubrics (directions) above the sealing sentence say that at the bishop's absence a priest may do the laying-on-of-hands. However, the resolution takes precedence over this rubric.

Many people feel that this sealing is anticlimactic and does not have the beauty and drama of the Prayer Book service of Confirmation. Such criticism is probably valid and one would hope that future revision of this rite would replace the "you are sealed . . ." statement with some version of the Prayer Book's "Defend O Lord this thy child . . ." prayer.

When all have been baptized and/or sealed, the congregation joins the clergy in the prayer of reception (top of page 30). It is certainly proper that everyone joins in this prayer because for too long the Church has forgotten the aspects of Baptism that include the fellowship, the blood brother/sister relationship, and the concept that those of us who have already received this initiation can still learn much from those now undergoing the rite. Too much of baptism has simply been the washing away of original sin.

The Peace is exchanged, and this act is also historically important since in the early Church the newly initiated candidates were greeted with the kiss of peace.

The rubrics at this point assume that the service continues with the Eucharist. This is another reference to earlier Church tradition where immediately after Baptism the new member was given his or her first Communion. Because of General Convention's resolution concerning Communion before Confirmation this ancient tradition can again be followed.

Should there not be Communion following the Baptism and laying-on-of-hands the service continues with the Lord's Prayer and a closing blessing.

It is important to read the additional directions and suggestions on pages 32 and 33, noting that the bishop ought to be the chief minister at the Baptism (of course he *must* be at the laying-on-of-hands) and the celebrant at the Eucharist.

Pages 33, 34, and 35 describe the forms for conditional Baptism, Baptism by a deacon, and emergency Baptism, all of which are self-explanatory.

The service of Baptism and the laying-on-of-hands attempts to bring back an earlier atmosphere in the Church concerning its initiation rites. At some time in its history, most probably in the 13th century, the Church changed its attitude toward Baptism. The initiation rite originally representing a combination and summation of a faith confession (creeds), death and resurrection (water of drowning and cleansing), repentance (John the Baptist), the coming of the Holy Spirit (Jesus' Baptism), and the fellowship of the community then turned into a ceremony which was almost solely designed to wash away the mark of original sin: "the World, the Flesh, and the Devil."

The Green Book service, while certainly recognizing our sinful condition, brings to light the elements of faith and repentance as well as the opportunity for the congregation to be a real part of the rite, thereby reflecting the blood brother/sister fellowship of the Church. As is true of so many of the "modern" Green Book liturgical innovations, the initiation rites are actually liturgical steps back into the Church's past in an attempt to resurrect some original symbols and values.

The new Baptism and laying-on-of-hands services are generally briefer than the Prayer Book Baptism or Confirmation services. There are two practical reasons for this. These services usually center upon children and young people and, although the church should not create its worship solely for the young, a service involving children should not drag on to the point of boredom. Another reason is that with the early Communion idea the Eucharist should follow both Baptism and the laying-on-of-hands. Brevity of both initiation and Eucharistic rites, enables this to take place generally within an hour of worship. It is of the utmost importance that the Eucharist, the central act of worship in the Christian Church, be the natural extension of the initiation rite. One's Baptism or Confirmation should be followed by one's first Communion. Such an occasion is a great celebration and can be a real point of reference in a child's venture toward personhood.

There are definite areas in need of revision in the serving of Baptism and the laying-on-of-hands. Some of these areas are practical ones specifically involving the laying-on-of-hands. Others are theological areas which General Convention needs to discuss and affirm or re-think. However, the Green Book rites of initiation pro-vide us with an opportunity in worship to express our basic faith and to renew our tradition as we renew our promises and commitments.

CHAPTER *3*

Ideas for Creating the Liturgy

One of the great ironies in the Episcopal Church today and perhaps the reason for much of the tension and so-called division present in many congregations is the fact that, while in the midst of a movement of liturgical innovation and creativity, many of us simply do not understand what *liturgy* is.

There are many definitions of liturgy, usually designed to fit whatever direction the liturgist wants to proceed in. Generally most definitions have a common element; namely, that what we do in a service should grow out of where we are and who we are. People who are pressing for liturgical renewal are saying that we need new ways of expressing where we are. "The traditional language and actions no longer represent me," they say. Another irony is that in searching for something "new" the liturgical movement has actually resorted to the earliest of Christian practices. The passing of the peace, for example, is one of the oldest symbols of Christian fellowship and unity. Another example is that many congregations, in response to seeing the Eucharist as a meal, now have replaced the Communion wafer with bread made by a parishioner. The use of oil in the liturgy is increasing.

Some churches have instituted the washing of feet and the signs of the charismatic movement: speaking in tongues, healing, etc., reminding us of the ancient practices and symbols.

In truth the liturgical interest has caused us to rediscover almost all of our symbols in an effort to make our services "relevant." *Almost* all. One of the oldest and perhaps most valuable symbol in Judaeo-Christian tradition is water. And we in the Episcopal Church have all but abandoned it. Many Baptisms, in fact, have been performed in which it seemed there was an effort made to hide the water. We sprinkle, dab, or trickle water on infants or adults, and we are very careful to wipe up afterwards. We rarely make much of the blessing of the water, and little if anything is ever mentioned about its power as reality or as symbol. In not stressing the symbol of water in Baptism we have missed a great theological and liturgical opportunity.

There are cultural as well as liturgical influences at work here, too. Emphasis upon initiation in the form of Baptism and Confirmation, varies with the condition of the Church. When the Christian Church was developing and still "illegal," initiation was a very important and dangerous thing. In the first hundred years of the Church's existence not many people were initiated. The ceremony was a very important event, both because of the religion's status in the eyes of Rome and because of the need for a larger and stronger membership. As the Church became accepted and established, Baptism and later Confirmation lost their individual value and these rites were often performed over masses of people; whole families, tribes, and nations were suddenly "christened." When the Church is "under fire" its initiatory side seems to pull together. When the Church is in fair weather it seems to show little concern about its process of admitting members.

In the 1950s the Church was popular and expanding. Those were relatively peaceful times. Membership was up but only in number, not in theological or liturgical importance. *Getting* members was important, not *how* or *why*. But in the late 60s or early 70s the culture was troubled. Now the Church as establishment suffers, and it needs a renewal of its birthright. The very reasons why there should be a Church at all must be reaffirmed. That reaffirmation can be seen in the beginning of a new interest in Baptism and Confirmation. When one's life is threatened, one naturally begins to think about new life and rebirth. Baptisms and Confirmations usually carry with them greater value for newly formed and struggling congregations than they do for older and more established churches. Our culture is forcing the Church to look at herself, and when that happens the Church falls back upon the initiation rites for strength. The question is: Will the strength be there?

Along with the cultural attitude of "church" and "religion" there are other influences upon the rites of the Christian. Just as the society in which the Church finds itself has its initiation rites so must the Church respond to, although not necessarily in order to sanction, those rites. Baptism should be one of the greatest responses the Church has to offer, but Confirmation or the laying-on-of-hands must also be presented as a highly valuable part of the Christian life. Just as Baptism says that children are a real part of the Church, so should the laying-on-of-hands say that commitment to the Christian endeavor is worth it.

For a young adult, society provides and often demands certain rites of passage which in reality are initiation ceremonies. There is the obtaining of a driver's license, for example, perhaps the most important social act for a person around the age of sixteen. There is the initiation into voting age, signing up with the Selective Service System, or turning twenty-one. These are some of society's initiation rites, and the Church must be ready to recognize them and to offer its own rites which hopefully give meaning to those of the culture. As society changes, the Church must keep her eyes open.

When these two influences—the growing interest in liturgical expression and the changing influences of a society—come together in the Church, exciting things can take place. Let us take a look at some of the ways liturgies can express our sacraments of Baptism and Holy Communion, drawing on our culture's symbols as well as the traditional religious ones.

Baptism

The symbolism of water has been neglected. The liturgy of a Baptism should focus on one particular theme (as any liturgy should) and the water theme is perhaps the best. Our society represents hundreds of uses for water. We swim, we bathe, we drink, we water our lawns, we wash our cars, we boat, and we fish. These are activities representing fun and cleansing and new life. We also pollute, drown, suffer tidal waves and flood. Water can kill as well as bring life. The Baptism service should show this. In the Green Book service there are ample opportunities for congregational participation; however, one cannot depend upon the form of a service to carry through the theme.

An effective method of presenting water is by showing slides depicting water images. Readings about water, sailing, and the oceans can be excellent settings for the services. There is great poetry as well as music written about water, which can also carry the theme. If we just sit down for a moment, we will discover a number of images and symbols that can be used in a service of Baptism.

One parish asked the people simply to dip their hands into bowls of water upon entering the church so that they might experience the feel of water. At the time of the blessing of the water the bowls which were at the entrances were poured into the font, symbolic of the congregation's investment and responsibility in this event. At another service a recording of the sounds of the ocean or of a waterfall was played as a prelude.

The service itself, especially in infant baptism, should be centered upon children and the actions should be made easily accessible to them. Invite the kids in the congregation to come forward, surround the font, and observe what is happening. At the time of the baptism, the water should be *used,* not hidden or wiped away. Some congregations are experimenting with having Baptisms at nearby lakes or rivers. Many young people, probably influenced by the growing fundamentalist groups, are insisting upon Baptism by total immersion. At any rate, it is obvious that the Church has not done justice to its sacrament of Baptism and especially in regard to the theme of water. The possibilities for renewal, liturgically and theologically, are endless.

One of the most unique and moving services at which to have a Baptism is Easter Eve. Historically this occasion, the eve of Christ's resurrection, was when the candidates for Baptism were presented. What better time is there than this to stress the beginning of new life! Along with the water image, themes of darkness and light can also be used to show the victory over death and the gift of a new beginning.

If there are no candidates to be presented for Baptism, members of the congregation can "baptize" one another. Such an act would not be a re-Baptism but rather a ceremony of baptismal renewal at which we rededicate ourselves in remembering and repeating our Baptism promises.

Baptisms should be public celebrations, held during the main service, not privately. The reason for this strong statement is that the service of Baptism (especially when the candidate is an infant), like the funeral service, is not so much for the person who is to be baptized as it is for the rest of us—the congregation. We are the ones responsible for the new member. We are the ones called upon to respond to this new brother or sister in love and fellowship. An infant is not responsible. Its godparents and the entire community must exercise their responsibility. And how can the Church family meet that responsibility if they are not aware of the Baptism? Surely there are occasions when private Baptism is necessary, but the rule should be that the rite be performed before the fellowship.

Baptism by immersion was mentioned earlier and, while many Episcopalians may recoil at the idea, there is great symbolic value in—for lack of a better phrase—"being dunked." In earlier times Baptisms featured the candidate being pushed under water three times, each time displaying a belief in one person of the Trinity. The dominant image here is that of drowning. Baptism represents a death to sin and a new life in Christ Jesus. The act of going under water, totally, is a real struggle for survival. The picture is a fight against the evil aspect of water—it can kill you—for the sake of the cleansing aspect. Baptism, in light of Christ's death and resurrection, says we can win the battle. But unless there is a strong allusion to the struggle (seen in the drowning), it is extremely difficult to see Baptism as a great victory. All this is by way of saying that immersion has its value. (This form of Baptism is still practiced in many Orthodox Churches.)

Water cleans us. Baptisms are also cleansing services. In ancient times a person who was to be baptized was stripped of his old clothes, anointed with oil (a kind of exorcism of the Devil), baptized (cleansed) in the nude, sealed with oil, and then given clean new clothes. We can learn two things from that practice. The first is the idea of *totality* as seen in the fact that the candidate for Baptism was completely without clothes, in a state of natural innocence, and was put totally underwater. The second thing is revealed in the anointing and sealing along with the new clothes. The symbolism is in getting washed and becoming clean.

Not long ago a controversial Baptism took place at a New York church which featured, among other things, a bathtub. Now it may be that that service overstepped the bounds of liturgical experimentation. However, using a bathtub in a Baptism is not as far out as one might think. The bathtub or the shower is a contemporary symbol for cleansing. If, in the planning of a Baptism, you were to think of all the symbols which point toward the theme of becoming clean, the tub would be a natural candidate. The use of a bathtub in a church service obviously has its problem, but the idea is good. Bring out the water/cleansing theme by using meaningful symbols taken from our everyday lives. Each congregation must search for its own meaningful symbols in order to express the themes of Baptism. A small mission on the edge of Lake Tahoe will have different Baptism symbols from a large downtown parish in Rochester, N.Y.

The naming of a person being baptized generally goes unnoticed. Names throughout the Hebrew tradition have tremendous importance. In many of our society's initiation ceremonies the candidate is given a special (and usually secret) name. The Baptism can offer us an opportunity to revive the value of names. When the sponsors present the candidate, infant or adult, for Baptism, they say the person's name. At that point in the service the congregation can simply repeat the name in unison, thereby symbolically approving the personhood of the candidate.

Sponsors: "I present Ellen Marie Johnson to receive the sacrament of Baptism."

Congregation: "Ellen Marie Johnson."

There is nothing magical about doing this, but the action allows the congregation to identify with this individual who is joining the ranks. Naming is important.

Baptism should evoke many themes and issues to be explored liturgically. In the past, we have seen Baptism only as the symbolic washing away of the filth of sin. But Baptism means much more. It means reconfirming our faith, dying and being born again. It means a congregation must recognize its responsibility to a new member. It means we are called to rediscover the dynamics of our initiatory rites.

An area of Baptism that the clergy often either overlooks or deemphasizes is the preparation of the parents and godparents. A cycle has been established: Because we have not recently stressed the importance of Baptism we have not put much effort into explaining it to the participants. Usually the minister will meet with the sponsors and the candidate, if he or she is not an infant, before the service, explaining what to do and when. There might be a short and rather vague presentation of what Baptism is, but such a presentation sometimes gets left out. Baptism has lost its value so we do not put much effort into explaining it, and because we gloss over it, the rite continues to be pushed aside. One cure for this is for the clergy to counsel seriously with the sponsors and parents long before the Baptism takes place and, at times other than the baptismal day, to present to the congregation further opportunities to investigate the meaning of Baptism and membership in the Church. One rarely hears a sermon about Baptism except at a Baptism service.

Another and related cure is for the laity to take this sacrament seriously. One small congregation in the Southwest individually presents the newly baptized member with a little gift: a card of welcome, a flower, a poem, a photograph of the occasion. In return, as the parishioners leave the church they are given small crosses to commemorate the event. Because of this awareness and investment by the sponsors of the baptized person and the entire community, an initiation is a "big thing" and not easily forgotten. Preparation for families, godparents, and the congregation is extremely important. Liturgical practices reflecting baptism themes, no matter how well done, cannot be as effective as they could be unless some preparation, some kind of exposure to those themes, has been experienced beforehand. In other words, what you do in getting ready for a service is as important as what goes on during the service itself.

No discussion of Baptism would be anywhere near complete without directing some thoughts toward the rationale behind infant Baptism. In the early Christian Church there was almost no infant Baptism. Later, when families were baptized together, infants began to be included. The practice of infant Baptism probably came as a response to the high rate of infant mortality and very strong doctrines of heaven and hell, redemption and eternal damnation.

"What happens to a baby who dies before being baptized?" people asked. "Would it be saved?" "Would it be Christian?" So the tradition started and has been strongly carried on by the Episcopal Church. But why have infant Baptism today? The main reason is that what the parents, sponsors, and Church community are all trying to say is: "We want you to have the best possible life and we feel that that life can be found through this Christian life-style. Therefore, until you are able to make your own decision about it we want to give you the chance to live as a Christian."

There is no magic involved. The infant is not conscious of what is happening. The parents and godparents are the ones who must hold the responsibility. The Christian community then presents its life to this child as he grows toward the time when he will make up his own mind. When that time comes he does not simply accept the promises made on his behalf at his Baptism, but accepts the responsibility of making a decision and a commitment. That is why godparents or sponsors are so important. When parents go about considering godparents, much thought should be given to the people involved. When taken seriously, as it should be, the role of godparent is an awe-filled one.

Communion

We have talked about how children learn and about early Communion. We have talked about preparing for

Baptism. Something should be said about preparing children *and adults* for a nonconfirmed child's reception of the Holy Eucharist.

To repeat an earlier statement, theological understanding follows participation. Children learn by doing and by watching others. They can consciously learn more than we give them credit for, even though they are not able to express their comprehension verbally. When one talks about preparation for early Communion, it must be stressed right off that this is not a ten-minute lecture by the Sunday School teacher or the rector. It should be an educational experience in which child, parents, congregation, and clergy all grow and develop.

To begin with, the decision to receive Communion or not, once the diocesan bishop has revealed his guidelines, is up to the child. Parents, clergy, and friends should never try to coerce the child for or against. The child should have as much input as he or she wants and the basic instrument for information should be the family with the clergyman as a resource. The decision should come out of a family discussion, but it must remain the child's decision. When is a child capable of making such a decision? That varies, just as children themselves vary. But parents who are in any way in touch with their children will know when the decision is a real one or not. Remember, none of us fully understands the Holy Communion; so don't expect full understanding from young children.

Children certainly can understand sharing and giving thanks. They can grasp a good bit of what sacrifice means too. Most children have a good idea of what remembering means. And they all will pick up on the Eucharist as a meal. The real difficulty involved in preparing children for Communion is encountered by the parents who must contemplate (some for the first time) what the Eucharist actually means.

A child's First Communion is a completely new experience mainly because the child has probably never experienced an entire service of Holy Communion—the pre-sermon exodus having taken its toll. Therefore, the first thing to do is go through the service, Prayer Book and/or Green Book, in a kind of instruction-manual way. Incidently, there is not a congregation in the Episcopal Church which would not profit from an instructed Eucharist at least once a year.

A discussion of the service should bring out the different themes: fellowship, sacrifice, sharing, eating and being nourished, bread and wine, etc. This is a good time to read the Bible passages recounting the Last Supper. And remember, the most successful symbol is that of the *meal.* Mention Passover, and in so doing you just might find yourself in the middle of the Red Sea, trying to explain unleavened bread and maybe even a little something about bondage and freedom. Children love stories and the story of the Last Supper is a beautiful one. The main thing is not to hit a seven-year-old with the theological concept of "real presence" first off.

When the questions begin coming in, be honest. If you do not know why they put water into the wine, find out. Ask a clergyman; don't make something up. If the children are going to take this sacrament seriously, the adults who present it to them must do the same. On the other hand participation in the Holy Eucharist can and should be an exhilarating experience. Along with being serious and reverent we can be happy and enjoy what is going on. Children should be told this. Because of attitudes in the Church about proper behavior during a service, most children are scared to death in church. They are afraid of doing something wrong. The invitation to Communion only compounds their anxiety. Because children are naturally transparent people they are not easily embarrassed and have not yet learned or fallen victim to such social intricacies as discretion or sophistication. Therefore, the sight of a young child almost paralyzed with the fear of dropping the sacred wafer must be one of the most unnatural scenes one can witness. Children as well as everyone else should know that unless we can be ourselves before God, we cannot be who we are anywhere. After all, "from [Him] no secrets are hid."

On the practical side, children should be encouraged to take the bread and wine like everyone else does. Some dioceses have given guidelines stating that the parents should take the Communion wafer, break it in half, dip half in the chalice when it comes by and then place the piece of wafer on their child's tongue. This act may have some theological or ecclesiastical meaning, but the main message it communicates is that the child is not really ready to do this thing himself. The whole idea of the General Convention's resolution is to say that the child is a full-fledged member of the Church. To turn around and physically undermine that thrust is unfortunate, to say the least. Children can feed themselves.

In preparing children for their First Communion, the relating of attitude is every bit as important as presenting practical pointers. On the day of their first eucharistic experience the attitude is what comes through loud and clear. For example, two parishes set a certain Sunday to be "First Communion Sunday." They both used this theme for their Church School and adult classes. Families were urged to talk about Communion and whether or not to participate. On the appointed Sunday they both had its "first communions." The results were remarkably different. Not that the results should have been the same, but the difference is worth noting. The first church had their usual Communion service with no emphasis on either the children or the importance of this great event. The second church focused on the children and the child in all of us. The first had Communion as usual, the second made a real effort to create an atmosphere of sincere excitement. Of course every Sunday cannot be aimed at the children and First Communions, but the attitude that second church produced was one in which the Eucharist was seen, as one child put it, as "really neat. I really liked it." From the first church came the response, "It was like the regular service—okay, I guess."

While this example is fictional, the attitudes expressed by it are not. For too many congregations the children's Communion is something to be got over with. Frequently not enough effort is put into making a child's First Communion a truly important event in his life. Children and young people can be very critical. They can sense when they are being genuinely accepted as full members and when they are not. The impression a child or young person receives from a Church service, specifically a First Communion service, can turn him on or off to future involvement. It makes all the difference in the world how the liturgy is done. What follows is applicable to Communion, Baptism, laying-on-of-hands, or any other liturgical event.

The clergy cannot and should not do it all. Lay people are beginning to take more active roles in the performing of the liturgy—passing the chalice; reading lessons, litanies, intercessions; giving sermons—but the real lay involvement needs to come in at the level of preparation and planning. Most clergymen are notorious procrastinators. Many clergymen simply do not have enough interest in liturgies. They are not moved toward any experimentation in the service. Usually the worship from week to week throughout the year is the same. However, the real tragedy in the liturgical scene is not the group who would rather not try anything new, but the people who say "yes" to some renewal of their worship only to turn right around and expect things to run smoothly with little if any input or preparation.

More often than not the preparation for a Sunday service gets done Friday or Saturday afternoon or evening. An idea or theme for a Baptism might come out of a worship committee. Everyone gets excited, different kinds of music are mentioned, samples of readings are discussed. And then on Sunday morning a few people are still frantically running around trying to find someone to read the Epistle or someone who can play a flute. Somehow the bread which was to be made and brought to the altar does not appear and the regular wafers must be used as a substitute. The guitarist was never called, so that idea had to be dropped. The young man who was supposed to find someone to read the Epistle ends up doing it himself and no one can hear him speak the passage that revealed the theme for the service.

What a letdown! Needless to say even with the utmost effort in preparation things will go wrong. But we rarely take the time to really practice and perform a service. If a Baptism, a First Communion, a Confirmation is going to be a big event, then it will take big work to make it so. If you are going to use a song or poem, the words of which are to be an integral part of the service, then the words must be available to the congregation, either printed in the bulletin or mimeographed and handed out. Worship is a dramatic thing and, like drama services, must be rehearsed. Time and effort, as well as creativity and imagination, are necessary ingredients to good liturgy-making.

And then there is the straw that can break the liturgical camel's back. Picture, if you will, announcement time during a service one week before the children are going to receive Holy Communion for the first time. The kids and their adult teachers, parents, and advisors have worked for three months getting ready for the occasion. They have made their decisions, they have created art to represent their feelings about what is to take place. The minister steps forward to call the congregation's attention to the coming week's events.

"And remember, next Sunday our nonconfirmed children will have their first opportunity to participate in the Eucharist. The service will be a bit different and some of you might not agree with what will take place, but I do hope you will plan to attend anyway." So, the best laid schemes . . . This slightly negative comment, made with the good intention of helping what was to take place the next Sunday, could have destroyed all the preparation. It is true that the congregation should be aware of what a service will be like, but to apologize for a service before it has been done is disastrous. "You probably won't like what you're about to see," is not exactly the phrase to use in opening a person's mind or heart.

But let us not draw too dark a picture. When there *is* some work involved, when a congregation *has* done its preparation, and when people *are* open to what might happen, a spirit of excitement can burst from a service. A Baptism can be the celebration of new life that it should be. A child's First Communion can be for him and for the entire community a moment to remember. But we cannot expect the clergy to do it all, nor can we say to the laity "it's your ball." These initiation rites, like any other services, take reflection and preparation. If one hour a week is going to be the focal point of a congregation's life, then a little elbow grease on everyone's part is necessary—but it's well worth it.

Finally, something should be said about how often baptisms and communions should take place. It used to be that any congregation that celebrated the Eucharist at its main service more than once a month was given the distinction of being "High Church." Fortunately, such bigoted terminology is on its way out. Within the past few years, the Episcopal Church has stressed the centrality of the Lord's Supper in our corporate worship. Consequently, more and more missions and parishes are celebrating Communion frequently. Helping some congregations is the brevity of the Eucharistic rites found in the Green Book. Now, a Communion Sunday that begins at 10 A.M. does not have to end at one o'clock in the afternoon.

Once a parish has started having Communion every Sunday they often find it anticlimactic to return to anything else. Some people argue that every Sunday is too frequent a schedule to maintain, and the service begins to lose its meaning much the way Morning Prayer has lost its significance. This is true in part, but the very action of the Eucharist is enough to keep it from becoming dull and uninteresting. It should be remembered, however, that the more often you have a Communion the more work will need to be done.

Children seem to be in favor of having Communion at

least twice a month and many would like to have it each week. Only a few out of almost one hundred second through ninth graders who were interviewed thought that Communion should be offered only once a month.

Now Baptisms are a different matter. There are quite a few factors involved in the frequency question here. Obviously, available infants and adults are not easily scheduled. In the case of infant baptism, the parents should check with the clergy as to when the best time might be. The clergy should continually remind the congregation of the importance of Baptism. The next factor involved is the bishop. All the proposed Baptism rites stress the fact that the bishop is supposed to be the officiant at the service. Bishops have extremely heavy schedules, and in larger dioceses or ones with only one bishop the visitations might be separated by a year or more. Now it is not necessary that the bishop be the officiant but the practice is historically valid and lends some real episcopal clout to the service. The problem might arise when some members of a parish are baptized by the bishop and others by the rector. It is the same Baptism but some people might feel that unless the bishop did it, it was not really valid. Some counseling and explanation would clear up such a situation.

One solution to the bishop's schedule problem would be for two or three parishes to have group Baptisms at the bishop's visit similar to group Confirmations. The local congregations would meet together at the largest church and the bishop would baptize and perhaps administer the laying-on-of-hands.

For some reason, too-frequent Baptisms seem to cause a kind of "Baptism backlash." Perhaps the church, like many other organizations, must keep its initiation ceremonies intact by making them relatively few and far between, giving the illusion that membership is something not casually performed. The idea of waiting a year for Baptism may not be all that bad. It would require a lot of work to keep up an interest in a yearly sacrament. On the other hand, the annual Baptism could be an initiation rite without parallel.

CHAPTER *4*

Confirmation/ Laying-on-of-Hands

The statement describing Confirmation as "a rite in search of a theology" has to be the understatement of recent Church history. Thomas Aquinas saw it as the preparation for the struggle with Satan. Reformation theologians thought it was something the Church could do without. In the Episcopal Church, Confirmation has been the "ticket" to Communion; a Christian Bar Mitzvah; the completion of Baptism; a short course in the history of the Episcopal Church; and an explanation of Church symbols, the Church year, the Communion service, etc. Confirmation is something that happens to you when you are twelve. Confirmation is sometimes "conformation." Confirmation is "when the bishop comes." Confirmation is classes you go through to become an Episcopalian or to brush up on some religious thinking. "Confirmation is when you get the Holy Ghost."

Confirmation has been and still is many of these things. Ironically, with all its vagueness and variety of interpretation, Confirmation, probably because of the bishop's presence, remains one of the highlights of a congregation's year. Add now to the already confused rite of Confirmation the fact that Baptism has been recognized by the Church to be total or full membership and the fact that nonconfirmed baptized people are allowed to receive Holy Communion and the result is an even more confused mess than ever.

People are saying that we are in the process of losing Confirmation. But what is it? What are we being threatened with the loss of? Historically, Confirmation grew out of thirrteenth-century ceremonies designed to prepare the adolescent for the future struggle against the forces of evil. Later feeling was that as one entered the years in which life became increasingly difficult there was a definite need to renew vows and to make that renewal public. There were probably many different kinds of these "Confirmation" services, and eventually they became more and more alike. The bishop became the central officiant and the laying-on-of-hands was used. After some time the Church accepted the rite of Confirmation. Our Book of Common Prayer describes the rite as "renewing the promises and vows of my Baptism, and declaring my loyalty and devotion to Christ my Master, (and) I receive the strengthening gifts of the Holy Spirit." And upon being confirmed "Our Lord provides the Sacrament of the Lord's Supper, or Holy Communion, for the continual strengthening and refreshing of my soul."

In the past seventy-five years Confirmation has stolen the fire (symbolized by the bishop's presence) from Baptism as the dominant rite of initiation in the Episcopal Church. What Prayer Book revision has attempted to do in the Green Book service of Baptism with the laying-on-of-hands is return to Baptism as the main initiation rite, placing Confirmation with Baptism so as to insure the candidate the chance to receive Holy Communion. This comes from a medieval concept that one's reception of Communion publicaly affirmed one's Confirmation. It was from this concept that Confirmation later came to be viewed as the ticket to Communion. At any rate, General Convention resolved that Baptism was an entire sacrament in itself and resolved that one could receive Communion before being Confirmed. This action has left us with a totally inadequate service of Confirmation and quite a superficial service of Christian commitment (p. 326 of the Green Book). So, what to do?

What to do is: a reevaluation of Confirmation. The Church has before it an opportunity to truly make Confirmation what most people thought it was—a rite of commitment. Baptism, especially infant Baptism, does not demand responsibility or commitment from the person being baptized. The responsibility and commitment at Baptism are really with the sponsors and the congregation. They must provide the person with a meaningful fellowship and love. Baptism gives the baptized person the gift of growing and developing in a Christian community as a full-fledged member. If the community has fulfilled its promises and vows and has given the baptized person love and acceptance, then the person should feel a need and a desire to respond to what the community of Christians has done for him and, furthermore, to make a real commitment to the enterprise. In Baptism the vows and promises are more statements of belief than they are statements of commitment. What Confirmation can be is the opportunity for the baptized member to enter into a concrete covenant, a real commitment, in response to what has been given him through Baptism. Such a rite would not complete Baptism but would be a response to that initiation ceremony.

Some years ago in Washington, D.C., a congregation was formed. It centered upon a contract of membership in which the individual who wanted to be a part of the congregation would draw up a contract that would include commitments of time, abilities, and money. An initiation ceremony was performed at which this contract was signed. In case the member found himself unable to fulfill the contract, he would present himself before the congregation, explain the situation, and resign his membership. This is a concrete example of taking commitment seriously. We need to do this same thing with the sacrament of Confirmation.

Most Confirmation classes never get around to the idea of making a commitment. We talk about why you should make a commitment, but we rarely get into a serious examination of what a commitment is, what it means, and what it costs. Let us fantasize for a bit on what Confirmation might be.

A young woman, age twenty-two, feels that she has come to a point in her life at which she wants to reconfirm her Baptism and to respond to what her membership has meant to her by getting involved in some sort of commitment to her Church and her Lord.

In consultation with her minister she would pursue some form of instruction, if that was needed, and might enter a course designed to examine in depth her response to the Christian Faith as presented to her through Baptism—a course in the study of commitment. Such instructional courses would be a part of the parish's Christian Education department and a person seeking "Confirmation" (or perhaps "Lay Ordination" would be a better term) would be urged to take these courses.

Again in consultation with her minister the woman would draw up a contract of commitment which would be as specific as she would want. Our Prayer Book definition of a commitment at Confirmation is "to follow

Christ, to worship God every Sunday in his Church; and to work and pray and give for the spread of his Kingdom." Our fictional young woman might be more exact in her commitment contract under the theory that the more specific a contract, the more important the commitment; the more vague the terms, the easier they are to rationalize away.

When the contract had been drawn up it would be published (similar to the publishing of wedding banns) at least two weeks before the service of Committment. Then on the prescribed date a ceremony would be conducted (called Confirmation, Lay Ordination, Christian Commitment) at which the young woman along with others, would read her contract, sign it, and receive the laying-on-of-hands by the bishop.

The moving force behind this fantasy rite would be from the individual. It would be a lay movement not unlike the Roman Catholic (now fast becoming ecumenical) Cursillo movement. A Confirmation under this model would not be something the bishop came around and did. It would be a decision and corresponding action on the part of a lay person with advice from the clergy. The bishop's laying-on-of-hands would be a symbolic validation of the commitment. Also under this model the bishop's main role liturgically would be to officiate at Baptism and celebrate the Eucharist, giving, by virtue of his position and tradition, the "fire" back to Baptism. This certainly would not mean that Confirmation would become a minor rite. On the contrary, being stripped of the stigma of Communion ticket, Baptism completion, and social nicety, Confirmation would be a significant celebration of renewal and commitment.

The Liturgy of Confirmation

Assuming that the future status of Confirmation or the laying-on-of-hands will move toward a commitment-contract model, let us look at some possible resources for a liturgy that would represent the rite.

Just as Baptism has a dominant theme in water, so Confirmation might use as its image the Covenant. There are many biblical references here—from Noah, Abraham, and Moses to Jesus' conversation in the Garden of Gethsemane. Comparable secular resources would be mortgages, business contracts, wills, and situations involving a transaction and the signing of one's name.

The importance of one's name in Baptism comes up again in a contractual concept of confirmation. There is something very binding about putting your signature on something. Signing your name is in itself a commitment. A person's signature represents him. So in a Confirmation service there ought to be a sealing of the commitment. This could be accomplished by the confirmand's signing the contract and then the bishop blessing the confirmand by administering the laying-on-of-hands and completing the service by the sealing with oil.

Present Confirmation services can use this same imagery by having the confirmand's name read to the congregation in his presence and, as in Baptism, the congregation would repeat the name. The confirmand would sign his confirmation certificate, receive the laying-on-of-hands; then the bishop would sign the certificate.

It is unfortunate that the Green Book service does not provide an adequate setting for Confirmation. One bishop remarked that, after repeating the phrase "you are sealed . . . ," he very often felt like he was working in a canning factory. Also the confirmand's response, "Is that all there is?" shows that this service needs some reworking.

And yet with an emphasis on the commitment-contract idea Confirmation could be an invaluable asset in the initiatory rites of the Christian Church. The possibilities for a great service of Confirmation are endless. A rite of commitment could combine the thrill of an initiation with the reverence and responsibility of taking upon oneself, with the help of the Holy Spirit, the task that is unique to Christianity—the dedication of one's life and effort to Jesus Christ. A revitalized service of Confirmation would fill a great void in the stages of individual growth in the Church. Here would be a chance to practice what we preach. We talk about following Jesus Christ as Lord and Saviour. Are we willing to enter into a covenant to that effect? Ask any bishop, priest, or deacon about his ordination and he will probably tell you that it is a frightening and exciting commitment. That kind of a commitment is what Confirmation should be—frightening and exciting.

CHAPTER 5

Conclusion

Back to the Children

So where does all this lead us? Baptism, Communion, and Confirmation point us to the fact that children and young people are members of the Church. But the real question is "Will we as adults take that fact seriously?" Because if we do then there will have to be a lot of re-thinking and reorganizing; a lot of mind-opening and patience will have to be displayed. For instance, if we really consider children to be real parishioners, as worthy as anyone else in the congregation of attention and acceptance, then we are going to have to practice that consideration. We are going to have to restructure our worship to include children, not send them out part way through the service. We are going to have to learn to live with children talking during a prayer or dropping their Offertory money. Perhaps we can begin to create liturgies which attract the attention of children as well as adults. For a long time our worship has been aimed almost exclusively at people over thirty or thirty-five years old. Now if we are going to take children and young people seriously, then we must do some changing of the aims of worship to include everyone.

Make no mistake! This does not mean that children are as responsible as adults or that when we say we will accept them it will be as mature, grown-up people rather than as the children they are. Often our "children's services" are simply performances by our cute little children —enjoyable, but not really important and not really valid worship. In order to change these attitudes it will take a conscientious effort on the part of every parishioner in a congregation to be open to what is happening.

Most of us would be shocked if the minister would announce: "Let us now sing the sermon hymn number 345, during which all the adults will leave and go to their classes." We must recognize that there will always be instances when children need to leave a service, but we need to know that children have been and continue to be affected and influenced by the little things we do, like having them leave before the sermon. A child brought up not to talk in Church will find that he has a hard time relaxing and being himself in Church later in his life. Children are usually more perceptive than we think. Our task as adults is to be as aware of how we treat children as the children are aware of how they are being treated.

Reemphasizing Baptism, preparing children for Communion, making liturgical changes to enhance the effectiveness of a service, offering a Confirmation with meaning, using the Green Book or the Prayer Book—none of these things in itself can create a thriving congregation, one in touch with its children's role in the Church. That can be done only by a spirit, a spirit of love. Not a vague love but a love that tries to understand others, their points of view, and your effect upon them. It is a love which asks, "Why can't a child (or anyone) drop a piece of bread at the Lord's table and not be embarrassed or afraid?" It is a love which asks, "Do I have a corner on the worship market? Can I share it with the whole congregation?" It is a love which asks, "Why do I think I am going to be offended?" It is the love of neighbor—even when that neighbor is a four-year-old boy or a fifteen-year-old girl who enjoys wearing blue jeans on Sunday.

A religious rite is made up of two basic elements: a visible symbol and an invisible power behind the symbol. In Baptism the symbol is water and the power is the Holy Spirit. Our approach to children in the Church is like a rite. We have the visible tools, the services and the little liturgical ideas by which we can attract their attention, but unless we have the Spirit, the Holy Spirit, we will not have attracted their hearts, and until we do our children will not really be a part of the family.

Afterword

There are a few issues which directly and indirectly influence and are influenced by Baptism, Confirmation, and Communion.

Not the least of these issues is that of the role of the bishop and his relationship to the priest. A situation which brings this issue to light is Baptism. It should be noted here that whenever one plunges into a discussion of bishops and priests one quickly finds himself in an analysis of "Apostolic Succession," an exceedingly vague area similar to the Trinity or the Atonement. What we are talking about when we discuss the roles of bishop and priest in regard to Baptism and the laying-on-of-hands is really what makes a bishop a bishop, a priest a priest, and why. One can get into a discussion of ordination and consecration, the laying-on-of-hands, annointing, etc., all of which can be interpreted either by saying that a bishop has a more direct line to the power or Spirit behind ordination or by saying that bishops and priests differ only in the administrative hierarchy and not in the spiritual one.

Because of the vagueness of what ordination and consecration mean and because of the vagueness of what bishops do and what priests do, there are some very curious and often quite defensive reactions between bishops and priests over a specific area of jurisdiction. For example, many priests regard Baptism as that occasion and ceremony over which the local priest exerts his authority and feel that a bishop who would come into a parish to officiate at baptisms would be overreaching his bounds. On the other hand there are bishops who are beginning to wonder what their roles are other than simply visiting congregations in order to confirm. Many bishops feel that any attempt to assign to a priest the authority formerly held by the bishop alone definitely threatens his (the bishop's) role. Such concern can be seen by the House of Bishops' reaction to the original Green Book service of laying-on-of-hands which allowed the act to be performed by a priest in the bishop's absence. That rubric was changed by the House.

Suffice it to say that while the relationships between priests and bishops can in no way be considered in danger of collapse, it should be pointed out that there are definite feelings on the parts of both priest and bishop about where their authority lies and where it needs to be reinforced.

What this book hopes to say is that the sacrament of Baptism needs to be revitalized in the Episcopal Church, and one way of recognizing its centrality is to have the bishop present and officiating at baptisms. Historically, the bishops did baptize and when it became necessary, due to growth of the Church, to give this role to others, then the local presbyter or priest began baptizing. The theory here was that the authority and "power" of the episcopate is the same as that of the priesthood; the issue became one of practicality. And there are still some practical problems concerning bishops and baptisms. However, the main point behind having the bishop officiate at baptisms is not whether he can do it better than the local priest but what emphasis he as bishop can bring to this initiation occasion.

On the other hand the suggestions this book makes in the area of Confirmation would seek to make the laying-on-of-hands a rite whose impetus comes basically from the laity in close relation to the local priest. The bishop's presence at what this book calls a service of Commitment or Lay Ordination would not have the same meaning as his presence now does at Confirmation. In other words what future initiation ceremonies might do is reverse the present situation to the point where the bishop's visitation would correspond with baptism and the local priest's role would concentrate more on a Confirmation or Commitment ritual.

Another communion and confirmation issue is age; at what age should a child take communion and when is it appropriate to make a personal decision toward a commitment?

Before the 63rd General Convention the age question was a simple one. You could not take communion until you were confirmed and the confirmation age was understood to be twelve. However after the Houston Convention the age range expanded. To begin with, the limits lay in the guidelines and suggestions of the diocesan bishop. One bishop might advise a lower age limit of six years. Another might leave the age totally up to parents, children, and the priest. Some suggestions ask that the child be able to walk to the communion rail in order to receive. Such advice seems to base the reception of the Eucharist on a physical ability, limiting the child even more than an intellectual restriction would.

The paramount factor in this issue should be the

child's decision and preparation, not his or her age. Obviously, then, when one talks about making a decision, one limits the age bracket of a child. This need not be the case. There seems to be no real reason why a baptized infant cannot receive the Eucharist unless the parents are bringing the child to the table simply to prove how young a person can be to take bread and wine. The responsibility for communicating an infant rests directly on the parents, assuming the bishop's guidelines have been followed. The seriousness of participation in the Holy Eucharist cannot be overemphasized. Children, parents, priests, and bishops will certainly vary, and different situations call for individual alternatives, but the value and importance of Communion are elements which must affect any decision whether made by child or parent, priest or bishop.

The 63rd Convention's resolution relative to the laying-on-of-hands talks about past confirmation age as a limit for receiving this new rite. However, if the future shape of Confirmation begins to resemble a contractual commitment model along the lines which this book suggests in chapter four, then the age appropriate to such an investment, while remaining open for individual circumstances, would probably be older than the "magic twelve years." There are no studies to prove when a person begins the process of serious decision-making but many sociologists talk about sixteen years old as being a lower limit. To place a limit on what age a person is capable of making a commitment, be it twelve, sixteen, twenty-one, or seventy would not only be difficult practically but shaky theologically. As in reception of the Eucharist, the emphasis in Confirmation should not be one of age but one of sincerity and awareness.

The big question surrounding the age issue is this:

"If you do not have some kind of limits, some kind of checks on the reception of the sacrament of Confirmation, then won't these rituals lose their meaning?" While this may be true, restrictions due to age or intellect are not the answers. What we must do to insure the validity and essential value of Communion and Confirmation—and any other rite for that matter—is to take the time and effort to explain these events to our children as best we can. A thing's value has never effectively been determined by restricting its availability but rather by using it well, respecting it in sincerity, and sharing it in love and hope. The Church's most valuable asset is its children.